To dearest Sherry

Blood Lines

This is very personal poetry therapy, freshly written, each and every word with my blood.

I hope you will get further insight of me and enjoy.

Thank you for being my mentor!

Ray
xxx

Blood Lines

Raymond Fenech

SandCrab Books

First Edition

SandCrab Books

www.canadacubaliteraryalliance.org/SandCrabBooks.html

Blood Lines
By Raymond Fenech

Editor: Manuel de J. Velázquez León
Layout and Design: Manuel de J. Velázquez León
Cover Design: Daniele Pitre

Printed and bound in USA
Library and Archives Canada Cataloguing in Publication

Fenech, Raymond
Blood Lines
Poetry

THE CONTENTS OF THIS BOOK ARE DESTINED FOR A MATURE AUDIENCE OVER EIGHTEEN YEARS OF AGE

ISBN-978-1-897475-85-0

To Pooch

October 1999 – February 2011

Acknowledgement

Manuel de J. Velázquez León (for writing the foreword)

Richard Ellis Archives Malta (old photographs of Malta)

Caroline Busuttil (photographs of St. Julian's Bay and The Immaculate Conception Chapel)

Maria Aurora Fenech, my mother, for lending me the photograph seen on the front cover showing her with my father in July 1943.

Kay Cardona, my English teacher in Form IV who guided me to my writing career.

My wife Angela for helping me with the choice of poems.

My beloved dog Pooch for patiently waiting on me during so many hours of work on these poems.

Table of Contents

Realizations – 41

Epilogue – 67

St. Julian's Bay

The Man of Many Shadows

The Man of Many Shadows

Ray Fenech's unique poetic sense breeds a diversity of shadows. Some are shed by southern Mediterranean sun through the kaleidoscope of cultures that crisscross in Malta, the magic space where the poet was born. Some are cast by Maltese ignis fatuus, ghostly memories of the islands' old, forgotten times. Sundry light sources produce miscellaneous shades: a poet of many shadows. To start the experience of reading his poetry, a brief quest by Fenech's varied cultural ancestries is required.

There are pale lights shining from the stone-frozen thoughts of those who built the Megalithic Temple of Hagar Qim, long before Stonehenge or the Egyptian pyramids were conceived. They are visible to Fenech with his natural talent to see the occult. They come in the whispers that Malta's evening sea breezes bring: spectral tales of Phoenician traders, Greek colonists, Carthaginian voagers and Roman legionaries.

The root of sadness in Fenech's poetry may come from the lament of maidens sacrificed to Baal thousands of years ago. His delicate eroticism may also be traced far back. As echoes to some of his best sensual lines, the reader might feel the doleful thoughts of a Carthaginian merchant who stayed in Malta pleased by the island's nice harbours and sick with love for a local girl of strange beauty who fell to the sword of her husband's servants. Long ago, the ardent whispers of the couple's nights of passion were erased by Mediterranean salty winds from the walls of a torn villa, but their feelings managed to remain in the race's memory down to many of these verses.

In about AD 60, Saint Paul was miraculously shipwrecked in Malta. His missionary work led to the conversion of the people of the islands to Christianity, thus starting a cultural and spiritual traition that has had more immediate influence on Fenech's life and poetry for there is faith in his verses. Besides the painful realization of ever-present tragedy in the world of the living, his lucidity envisions promises beyond sunset mist, fresh avenues to tread yonder Mediterranean horizons. Hope is a constant in these poems, felt and suggested rather than told, for that is the poet's mission: insinuation.

Such are the fundamental sources of this strange book. When their time came, they bloomed and fructified. Fenech collected the clusters on the vines and fermented their juice with his intense living experience. Here is the offering, warmed under Mediterranean starry nights.

First, is the poet's initiation, the novitiate of his spiritual quest. Poems here deal with his early world explorations as a thinking, living being. Like Whitman's child, Fenech goes forth in the original venture of naming a world that is thus reborn with the creative might of his words. There are crayon paintings of love inaugurations sketched with a naturalism that hurts the flesh: cherished erotic memories, vivid, vaguely preserved until they are resurrected in a poem. Such is a passionate affair later seen, in agony, dispensed to someone else. Once and again, there is the relived episode of losing innocence, always thrilling –here with particular intimacy–, sometimes a retell of somebody's experience, occasionally paralleled and inlayed into bedtime tales. Now and then, the poet looks from a distance, events rushing by, a whole life at a glimpse frozen into the magic of a poem, fast passing seasons in the realization and understanding of boundaries between the allegedly real and "reality".

Conscious as he is of the inevitable fatalities of memory, of the possible futility of human hopes for immortalizing what is felt, what is lived, Fenech cherishes dreams of preserving loved odours in an ideal magical box. Perhaps that is why his country is always there, in lovely, well-crafted word images, as if to save from the disasters of time what he has seen in different moments and spaces of his life in Malta. Therefore, he retrieves memories of childhood in class, vivid remembrances that quickly become past, like his prised child painting of Roman wars, as gone and dead as events of 2000 years before when Hannibal crossed the Alps. Perhaps, after all, one of the tasks of the poet is recording beauty for posterity and he is only a witness who tells and thus saves the eternal youth of a mannequin, in its recorded self-controlled, calmed state, in its most cherished quality; it's immunity to pain. Here, the poet's creative powers are at its best. The magic of his might deserves the metaphor of a ghostly force.

Then, Fenech turns into a witness, a spy of whatever is hidden under the film of sun dust that covers every day's acts, under the frozen crust of certainty. That is the case of Ray's accurate depiction of love for life, respected in its natural condition, though humanized by benevolent feelings. Central themes are mind's creative might and the realizations of mortality, but always within the perfumed hope that comes from faith. So it is when he reveals the painful legend of the redwood tree, sort of a pagan myth underpinning a most sacred Christian belief. There are terrible moments when the reader is sternly commanded to attempt and explore fresh possibilities while imagination fills the crevices of the unknown and illuminates the paths left behind, urged to muster the courage and the will to proceed because that is the route to the only possible realization.

This uncanny spirit is again present in poems like "Light After Dark" in which illuminated and illuminating metaphors drift on the light of human knowledge, in the midst of the vast darkness of the unknown, and one can feel the light within coming from behind consciousness. However, even for the blind there's "a shade of grey", for all is in the mind. In a more down-to-earth vision of despair overcome, the poet starts travel towards light coming out of sickness, pain and the certainty of death in a hospital bed. The journey is paralleled to life flowing back from the fridge into the red roses in a vase, into the warmth of his wife's hand. Again and again, salvation by love is possible, we are told by this poet of pain and hope.

Now and then, windows open into gardens of what could be termed 'local colour', poems in which life in the fishing village is masterly depicted, human actions are painted in full, the flashing beauty of a passing woman is recorded for posterity while the poet senses with his tools into her reverie. Like a grain of sand in the wind, he turns into a witness of the universe, significant in his insignificance since all happens by and, perhaps because of his presence.

The last act is marked by a sadder vein: painful realizations of the world's change and decay prompted by agonizing signs or just by memories of a better past. Such is the selling of his mother's house, for one-hundred years his family's residence. There, the poet can hear the voices of countless generations while in the yard cicadas and lizards continue their timeless existence beyond life or death. Even then, there is still hope that the souls of the past, trapped in the house, will survive despite the move.

Malta and the fishing village where Fenech was born become protagonists of their own drama. Beauty reigns while the soul slides from multitudes of poppies to nightfall, a nightfall that slowly floods everything with its grey decolouring of the world until their red lips only remain in children's dreams. However, the tide of sadness rises again with the growing loss that results from the coming of modernity, with cash becoming more important than people's feelings. A witness of social transformations in the brief span of his life, the poet suffers. Receding past remains as memories upon previously insignificant objects, like a hat forgotten in the attic, while growing consciousness of mortality and decay turn the wrecked boat of youth into a cage of sad memories.

In this way, the last episodes close. Fenech has gone from the loss of innocence to the discovery of the world; then, the balance tilts over the fragility of human life, barely sustained by the renewal of hope, and slides towards the revival of faith, even if it is to be found in the grey shades of dusk. The legendary journey of the mind finishes its cycle where it started, in Malta, where timeless sea currents converge in verses of luxury: a poetic experience never to forget.

Manuel de Jesús Velázquez León, PhD
Lecturer in Studies of the English Speaking Cultures
University "José de la Luz y Caballero"
Holguín, Cuba

Spinola Bay

Initiations

Fleur

I was a child when I first fell in love
though immersed as you were in vanity,
I had visions of magic and mystery;
vivid full of illicit desire.

But now time has fled, and I know not where
our promises – castles in the air,
made in the bedroom, when trembling fingers
explored our naked shame – we lingered.

I traced your curves with breathless lips and called
your sexy name a hundred times in vain.
You only used to laugh at me and feign
not to hear when I asked you to marry me;

you dipped your fingers deep in me unfazed,
yet your deep blue eyes could not meet my gaze.

First Night

How I still remember you
now as you cross my path
swaying your tall elegant body
your hair in pony-tail beating a rhythm
like the last samba we danced in Brazil

how your flanks still move
and I thought all was forgotten
for even now your buoyant breasts are still
the same where I had buried my blushing face
before you mounted my inexperienced erection
and rode me into light and dark
until I was dry and sweating
and after couldn't stop wanting you

how we groaned in ecstasy and I thought
this love was surely eternally sealed
and I could not forget
my heart refused to obliterate this memory
until I saw you flirting with another
whispering sensuously your tongue probing his ears
as you had done on our first night

how my heart missed the rhythm
and my chest ached from affliction
and to this day though I've ridden
to many a light and dark
I still remember.

A Biography

The old grandfather clock chimes the *Ave Maria*.
When his grandparents died the sound became a mental strain.
It was sold in an auction; he will never hear its refrain.

His uncle's summer residence was a lighthouse.
With his cousins, as a child, they chased the shadows away.
Dusk was an adventure; only stars lit their way.

For years his father was a Franciscan novice. Sex was a sin.
Sunday mass with cousin Elsie was a passionate quest.
Hands folded, he reached with his fingers to fondle her breasts.

In South Africa he lived in a hut with the poor.
It was at the peak of youth, when he was moving at full steam.
There, all hopes and aspirations vanished like a dream.

The house where he lived, where he would want to die
smelt of the past, when all was well and he was young.
There, garden ghosts whispered advice in silent tongues.

When he was assigned to Bosnia, he became immune to fear.
Being a Red Cross volunteer required certain courage.
When it was over, he was no longer afraid of carnage.

He was thirteen and naked. He did not know he was beingwatched.
His cousin Ralph walked inside his bedroom like a streak.
His eyes spoke clearly. Ralph was strong and he was weak.

His first "love" was homosexual. He was raped by pleasure.
When eighteen, Celia came giving him the first French kiss.
When his tongue inside her churned up juicy bliss.

Celia had the loveliest eyes he had ever seen.
Her lips sensuous, when she spoke his eyes filled with tears.
Her breath slid softly inside his ear like an elixir.

As a child his favourite companion was a piece of cloth.
When frightened he covered his face keeping the world outside.
He grew violent. Tchaikovsky's 1812 was as if war was in his mind.

Personality disorder struck. He fought against himself.
Until reality and fear drove him insane.
A clock chimed the *Ave Maria*; he will never hear its refrain.

Broken Innocence

The door was a safety barrier
against grown-ups and religion.
When I exploded and couldn’t stop,
it collapsed the walls of my prison.
We both knew what we wanted,
we both got what we had dreamed about
and ate each other sweetly.
Unconscious with pleasure we saw through life,
and discovered a shade of grey.
Then, rains fell abundantly outside
and lightning shook us awake.

Endless Summers

How I dream about us going back in time
to those endless summers,
when time seemed to stand still,
as if waiting for us to catch up;
and when we watched sunsets
they were like fired mirrors
full of our passion and desire.

Then, it was forever, or so it seemed;
there were no signs of pain or fear,
both of us sweated for want of each other
our fingers slipping often into the unknown,
exploring forbidden crevices ...
hoping these were the ultimate moments,
until we lay side by side breathless
trying to come to terms with what seemed
lawless, immoral, or even a crime;
our love was berserk.

I remember you in your tight blue shorts
which you wore so teasingly to provoke
showing off your suntanned curves.
You are in my mind like an indelible portrait
only yesterday was thirty five years ago.
Now, I wonder about your satin black hair,
if it still flows down to your naked waist,
if you still swing your head from side to side
like a flowing samba rhythm?
Often, you used to catch me
from the corner of your eye
and you would sadistically smile,

pull your hair to one side
with your delicately thin fingers
letting it flow onto my bare chest.

I inhaled your perfume
as if it were the essence of life,
or an elixir of immortality
never daring to wash it off
until you returned, night after night
in secrecy and silence,
while shushing my enthusiasm,
afraid our love would fade like the porcelain moonlight
in which we basked so often,
until it turned invisibly pale.

No one knew of our secret love then,
of our illicit desire to rest in each other's arms
spending those youthful nights,
until they turned grey with age.
when we touched, it was like an electric shock,
our hearts beat so fast I often thought
the thumping would give us away.
Your sighs and my sighs seemed so loud,
too loud to stifle into the darkness.

Until the world around us caved in unexpectedly
and we broke apart into divided worlds.
How I would like us together to go back in time –
if it was not for the fear we would linger on
perhaps, even choose different paths, different ways
never to return, never to be what we are today.

Falling in Love

I fell in love a million times
day in day out
each time I thought:
this is the one.

The Dancing Bag

From stillness
the gentle breeze
inflates it with air,
like a heaving chest
lifting it in a spiral
of pirouetting leaves.

Then, the silent dance:
the unfurling rush
swirling across,
up, upwards into twirled wrinkles
vacuumed into autumn's dried whirlpools;
this rustling flow takes off,
a ballerina performing a *grande jeté.*

Growing With the Shadows

It took giant steps from that spring,
when the waddling child,
like a rubbery doll screamed in excitement,
tongue wagging inane language.
At times he seemed surprised,
and halted to listen to his own voice
emitting sounds like the many that came
from cages in the zoo.

His skin, like a wetsuit,
warm, cold, or flaming,
even in winter's draggling shades,
when old witches were tied to wheelchairs,
as if grounded following confrontation
with the fairy godmother's walking stick.
Angel's wings were in his feet,
at the sight of a gap-toothed mouth
grinning evil in a wrinkled face.

The teacher's shadow on his desk,
her powdered face with red lips
he'd have liked to kiss
towered against a dark blue sky;
she sat on her chair, legs slightly apart,
white laced panties and suspenders showing.
The fall came with tramps
lighting bonfires to bake chestnuts,
an aroma of burning wood
that teased his hunger;
the coal like lava in cauldrons,
an aura of flickering red and orange,
announcing Halloween and Christmas.

The green colour of fields
became brown, then tinted white,
many times, over and over again
until the scenery existed only on video;
the bulldozers and cranes came
to abolish the fir trees,
to build concrete blocks
that seemed to have grown from marbled roots.

The days of the boogeyman were over
the house of the cruel witch lay in ruins –
strangely there was no evil there.
The only signs of the fall
were in the garden shop,
littered with dry decapitated leaves,
shadows in half grey light.

Forgotten Fairy Tales

He lost his innocence with his first orgasm ...
All bed time stories –
escaped through his sleep,
soft like the feathers in his pillows,
or the invisible clothes worn by the naked king.

The woman wore shorts under her skirt
before she threw herself off the city entrance ...
And he must have forgotten how Alice looked
when she slipped down the rabbit's hole,
into the dream world from which there was no exit.

He fell in love with his neighbour's wife ...
Then came King Arthur
who tripped on Excalibur
betrayed by Guinevere and Sir Lancelot:
the sword sank with chivalry ages ago in the river.

His first love was his cousin ...
He had forgotten all about Greek myths
the flying unicorn, Pegasus,
on whose back he had flown through many stormy nights,
when grown-ups feasted, and parties were censored
and after 7 p.m. was curfew time.

Erotic dreams were soaking wet with frustration ...
Childhood dreams were now vague
and children no longer believed
in Santa who was framed with rape:
or Dickens' three ghosts of Christmas.

The Primary School Classroom (1965)

Lightning flashed. All pupils were whipped awake.
Shiny arrows flew across the sky thick with candy floss.
The voice was smothered in dumbstruck stillness.
The teacher was no superman. He was frightened and cross.

The Alps closed in. Hannibal marched on plastered walls.
Death, blood red, drowned in spoils of Roman wars.
Among the prize winning watercolour paintings was mine.
Depicting a gory battle, where soldiers fight until they fall.

Tempus fugit. The old carob tree was like a hunchback.
It whispered something I couldn't catch, from the past.
I listened hard, but the breeze blew in gale force winds.
And the tune changed from rock to rap and talking fast.

Years are fossilized like humans immobilized.
I travelled, bought souvenirs to remind me of mystery:
Since I was born, men have been to the moon and back.
Suddenly it's the year 2000: the present becomes history.

My Box of Scents

I want to lock up every scent that ignites a sensation in a box:
childhood's scent of the first rains flooding my Wellingtons;
lemons, with early morning air reeking of fresh eggs;
my father's *Old Spice* aftershave at the crack of dawn;
my mother's favourite perfume, *Anais Anais*;
fresh heather on a cold breeze before Christmas;
deep fried *Imqaret*[1] on the coldest of a long wintry day;
chestnuts, baked on burning wood in rusty cauldrons;
thousands of books in a library where silence is centuries old;
sea spray, fresh from the milk of its rising crests;
toasted bread, fresh tea leaves and fried bacon and eggs;
freshly cooked coffee beans with cloves and cinnamon;
the clean saw dust in my father's workshop;
my beloved's sweet smelling skin after a passionate embrace;
a storm with gale-force winds that gives breath an extra flavour;
my mother's oven baked macaroni on every feast day;
fresh fish covered with seaweed in a wicker basket,
so each of these ghostly scents will become immortalized ...

---

[1] *Imqaret* (date sweets) are traditional Maltese sweet made from dates and various other ingredients available all the year round.

The Mannequin

I thought the mannequin
was throwing me a kiss
from its white pouting lips,
virgin, that cannot sin;
its plastic discoloured by light
into a greyish yellow
like a deadly vampire.

Time moved in the fading sky
locked in a prison without bars,
the day's metamorphosis,
where seasons change but never die.

It had been stripped bare
to its very skinned shyness.
A boy made vulgar gestures
when his mother wasn't looking,
but it stood there unmoved, unfazed,
envied forever for its eternal youth,
immunity to pain, silent wisdom.

The Ghost in the Ink Pot

The ghost in the ink pot
guided my hand
into the yellow light
of the desert,
then into the mirage
where the water
welled in my eyes
like a fountain
of crystals.

Suddenly I was
outside a world
of dimming lights
where the sun was masked,
by damask,
and when it tired
simply laid down to rest,
cooling its fury
into the sea
sizzling as it sank
deeper into the deep.

The ink pot's ghost
leaves his mark
like the Scarlet Pimpernel,
in pulsating handwriting
in words from within;
flowing senseless,
or meaningful,
with calibrated rhythm
or rhyme, like music,
sound spilling,
splitting silences.

Fishermen cleaning and preparing their fishing nets for their next trip.

The Witness

Death of a Stray Cat

It moves slowly squatting on its hind legs
eyes glimmering yellow agony;
this is the last
of its nine lives already spent.
The cold spits its anger in convulsive rage
like crystal bullets the hail
unloads, pelts its rib cage.
Its last meow sounds
like a new born child.
Smoke from chimneys bursts,
forming breath-like clouds,
vanishes into freezing lights.

It searches for shelter,
shakes gelid water from its paws.
It eyes the high wall wishfully,
but its swift perfect agility
is only in the distant past.
Darkness closes in.
There is no sound or stir.
The rain drizzles on.
The milk in its plate untouched remains.

Birth of a Mosquito

Buzzing it slipped out almost transparent
from beneath azure space;
razzing at its inability to fly

it fizzed with long proboscis,
beyond the day's quivering laze,
dazzled by cascading colours:

its vibrant jazz increased.
It zigzagged
like a Harrier jet racing its engine:

then, as if it remembered
it zipped above water,

zapped out into space with a fulminating blaze,
that was soon part of an orchestrated buzz.

The Legend of the Red Dogwood

A legend speaks about the red dogwood,
how during a certain crucifixion
so gigantic, tall like an oak it stood,
it served as a cross for His affliction.

This destiny worried the tree so much
that He sensed its unhappiness deep inside,
and assured it that He bore no grudge,
He said it would bear witness to His plight.

"Never again will you grow huge and strong
from now, you will be slender, twisted and bent,
your blossoms like a cross, two petals long,
two petals short - pray mankind will repent.

In the very centre of the outer edge
on each of your petals, nail prints will appear,
rusty brown, blushing, crimson, stained with red.
Far, far away from evil men must steer.

And in the centre of each of your flowers
will be a crown of thorns for all to see,
recalling this man and His last hours,
and you hence forth, from sorrow shall be free."

The Electric Storm

Tonight the sky is an electric dream
flashing its giant camera with all its might
with an unceasing photographic mania.
Children hide their heads under the pillows
and parents pray to St. Barbara[1]
from fear of such magnificence.
Electric dreams pass quickly into impregnated skies
like youthful fantasies faring unexplored oceans
where many a Columbus's hopes sank.
November is the month of the dead,
when flower shops sales are at their peak
when Catholics burn thousands of candles
hoping to save souls, even those already lost.
And this feast of lightning sounds
like sacrileges fireworks, or angry Gods,
telling us we behave like the Pharisees,
giving us a last chance for eternal life.

---

[1] When there are thunderstorms, it is common tradition of the Maltese especially of the elderly, to pray to St. Barbara for protection from the damage that lightning can inflict on their homes.

Inside the Bare Wall

Enter inside the bare wall
where the white room swallows shadows.
Close the file of your past
roll fast forwardly into the mist,
wait until it clears,
fade into the shade of trees.
Now, some long forgotten love
has fallen from your thoughts.

Ignore heartache – read Blake:
imagination is not a state
it is the human existence itself.[1]
Open your hands like a sail
let the breeze push you forward;
grit your teeth, the somersault complete.
Orchestrate your singing with birds,
do not be afraid to flirt.
Jot down the music in your brain
and juggle with the notes;
dance, twirl like a whirlwind,
spinning, pirouetting.

In the quiet you can blink back
your tears, hear yourself think.
Become a Buddhist, cultivate Chinese cactus
beat a rhythm on an African drum,
tam tira tam tam tam, tira tam tam tam ...
let your hands fetch jungle sounds,
until the damping dew is dry
and stormy communications cease.
Now love will not need riches,
nor radiance in precious stones.

---

[1] William Blake.

The Mountains of Mourne – An Impression

The
sheep
stand
dotted grey
against a mantle of green.

The tips of mountains
hidden-like,
Jack climbing the beanstalk,
breaking
through clouds; mists, that hang over
from never ending skies,
menacing, threatening rains
that never seem to fall.

The sheep dogs break loose, yelping
into a run, tongues hanging,
rounding up the phosphorescent sheep
as twilight comes
like a spectral myth of romance
eternal salmon pink
which has kept the night at bay, since
days of yore and legends.
Now, the sheep are all gathered
unlike my raving thoughts,
vagrant tramps of mischief and wonder.
I leave these mountains
blushing with rhododendrons afraid
I will die
and never be back here again.

Light After Dark

For us light after dark is not
like the aurora borealis;
it's not the day's beginning
on the edge of the horizon or on
a windowsill: an eye peeping over
a mountain, bloodshot from
too much opening and closing;
it's just a light within
that does not light up a room
but lights up a world
like no other light can do.

Light after dark is seeing
life's vitality through luminosity.
We are all children of light or darkness
born after sunset, or sunrise
when the day is on its way,
it's no matter we are blind
there is always a shade of grey.
It's all in the mind – if we lack one sense
it's likely another is sharpened instead,
and darkness is cut by a sword
that flashes in the night,
illuminating the mind from behind.

Light after dark is clean,
like cutting an eye-ball in half
without inflicting pain;
we cannot feel what we cannot see:
in one's life there is only one light within

bathing in a moon-filled pond,
that we see better with sightless stares.
But it doesn't matter, not really –
we recognise all truths far better
like they were written on stone
and we can see with touch,
all's hewn in our other senses;
therefore we do not crave for vision –
it comes to light after dark.

Operation – Travelling Towards the Light

To my lovely wife, Angela

Eyes travel ahead
like spotlights;
lasers fencing with darkness
and the unknown.
On this cold metal bed,
identity is on a plastic bracelet
and silence converses with itself.

I am no longer within
and the pain is gone.
For the first time
I am at peace
in a waking deep sleep.

Then a light appears
through closed lids,
blood red like a sun.
A sea in dreams
leaks through my eyes
staining pillows.

Time freezes in my veins.
The Siberian cold chatters
with death until it leaves the room.
But only this time.

Life flows back
from the refrigerator
into red roses in the vase,
and the warmth of my wife's hand.

The Girl on the Gozo Ferry Boat

Her stare into a void of blue,
a sea of salt, breezes blown,
unceasing, wave after wave of white foam.

She stood there,
a magnificent specimen of the human race,
half naked, suntanned flesh,
hips bare, curves showing
each time teasing winds rose.

Her face, shadowed profile,
her gloomy pensive mind,
withdrawn, aloof,
in search of something, happiness?
Joy is an elusive dream.

Platonic Love

Beautiful as a Greek statue,
her jet-black hair hung in satin long curls
eyes beaming wide like a black onyx.
Only her voice spoilt the synchronisation
of this artistic creation:
it was coarse, masculine,
like a transvestite.

Married but naïve,
she was a virgin in more ways than one.
Never had a proper orgasm,
simulated in a forced effort to express
pleasure merely from a sense of duty.

She was stuck in stagnant boredom,
often reflected in her nail biting habit,
as she watched with dreamy eyes
a colourless world go by,
beneath her confined balcony.
It was at times like this their eyes met,
fleetingly, in one single passionate glance
that often took their breath away.

That was all there was to their love affair.
It was enough; their eyes said everything
from poetry to pornography.
When she parted her lips, he parted his
and their tongues spoke in flicks
of silent conversation.

Their love was condemned to this torture of make-belief;
of turning their heads away
when their eyes were about to speak,
when their smiles almost risked their hands waving kisses,
and their sighs were about to become
too loud and clear to hide.
This love was different from many others,
a love so perfect it could not survive.

Sunrise of a Fishing Village

The fishing village comes to life
at the first light of dawn
with *Pawlu*, the fisherman shouting:
"Lampuki friski, hajjin, hajjin!"[1]
Scaring away the last shadows
as they were sucked back into the pebbled beach
where they run, scurrying away
to hide with the crabs in dark crevices.

The radio news is all about politics and crime,
how one MP denigrated another,
how a burglar burst into a house,
killed an old woman suffocating her with a plastic bag.
Today the burglar is a repented poet
free as the wind and back in circulation.

Pawlu hollers in his high pitch voice:
"Lampuki friski, hajjin, hajjin!"
It's all about the fresh *lampuki, vopi* or *sparli,*[2]
it's all about the bulging bright eyes,
glaring up from amongst the deep green seaweed.
The fresh smell of the sea and the salt,
his *luzzu*[3], *Santa Maria*
and the fishing lines that earn him his living.
Who cares about politicians and their lies?
Who cares about all those self-centred snobs

who have never seen *Pawlu's* fresh *lampuki*?[4]
It's all there, the truth you want to know,
the life you want to live, its true meaning:
a sun rising from the yellow pebbled bay,
red, a shy apologetic face,
with each new day of human warmth,
as the shiny armoured fish quiver in the wicker basket
blissfully captured in a time capsule.

---

[1] Fresh Dolphin fish, alive, alive!
[2] *Lampuki* (Dolphin Fish) *Vopi* (bogue); *Sparli* (Annular Seabream).
[3] Traditional colourful Maltese fishing boat.
[4] *Lampuki* (Dolphin Fish)

To Gulliver "the Stuff that Dreams are Made of"

I live the dreams you dream
in wasted night-long sleeps.
Death rather than that!
Without sleep, they say,
you live very little.

Like Dante's "Divine Comedy",
dreams arouse fantasy.
Nightmares come to life
in night's deep shadows,
crawl lightly into the feathers
of your soft pillows
those you bang every morning
while hating yourself for remembering
or forgetting dreams.

Fatigue and rest are opium –
close your eyes
and it's all over for that day.
Sunset, fast-forwarded is within you:
enter the world of adventure!
Sunrise is folded in a curtain,
at the command of your alarm clock.
Open your eyes, look inward,
there is no rest in slumber,
only in dreams.
The child becomes Hercules,
Ursus, Ulysses, Perseus;
he fights, never dies –
under the sheets.

This is why I fly
whilst you fall, breaking your bones;
I see red in the darkness of anger,
white in refrigerated ice,
black in oblivion,
yellow in cowardly escapades;
but what the hell?

Like Gulliver
I live the dreams you dream
and deal with far worse monsters
than your everyday office routine.
I am not safe like you,
when you wake shaken by a nightmare;
for all the time my life is at stake,
whether asleep or awake,
like snowflakes, it can all vanish
on touch down with the lake.

A Grain of Sand

I am like a single grain
of sand in a desert –

blown about by winds
onto several pathways –

effecting people's lives
in miniature proportions –

threatening to blind
when angered –

or serving as a soft warm
bed on a sunny beach –

the wind is my friend
the sun fires my soul –

I am time's worse enemy
when I am used to measure it –

I am golden like a star
without a shine –

this grain of sand does not feel pain
to think, all that worldly pain –

is buried beneath this grain
of sand in the desert.

Spinola Palace

Realizations

HD's First Blood

Plants don't get cancer – we do
mine came like a lightning bolt
split the darkness of self-assurance
and left my soul in crystal shards.

The first blood is drawn with the injection of burning chemo

As I look at the white walls around
there are bloodstains full of human effort
each drop tells its own story of too many
white or too little red cells.

It will burn my spirit eventually and my hair will fall out

I could read it in their faces:
"this cannot happen to me",
just like I used to think before it happened
but it will cure after I've died a dozen times.

The chemo comes in lollipop orange colour and transparent gin

Every drip is an ocean
like a drop of TNT that travels
through the sea of blue on the wall
into mapped veins and blurred vision.

Hearing your heart beat for 144 hours of drip

Just as the light diminishes
the leaves of the flowered curtains turn grey
into a nauseating smell of detergent soap
as the nurse walks in to check my pulse.

The last remaining strength is killed, the price for more sunsets

Two doctors discuss the *Da Vinci Code*
the room is wiser but I prefer *Harry Potter*
with each passing hour this elixir
of life kills more hair follicles.

The sun seems so far away – All Souls' Day is in church bells

I am not who I was before
but what I will be tomorrow
after the long sleepless night
and forgotten dreams about Captain Nemo.

Only now I notice the preciousness of the dark outside.

The Sword Lily (Gladiolus)

To my father who loved Sword Lilies

They have grown unfailingly each year
for many years since your green fingers
planted the bloodless bulbs,
that grow pink like the inside of a vagina.
Too many years to remember,
too many events you were part of.
Smiling through your pain.
The contortions of your mouth
were even more terrifying on your handsome face.
The Sword Lilies you sowed
seem like you're re-visiting each time they grow.
Now every spring I expect to see them
to see you in them pain-free.
Perhaps a few more springs will pass,
and when they fail to grow,
I'll know you are calling me.

In Memoriam for My Father

The nurse asked me for his clothes:
a white shirt, a black tie,
black trousers and socks.
No need for shoes;
he was stripped
as I waited outside.

The shirt, which used to be a perfect fit
hung loose at the neck,
caved in at the chest;
the tie's knot was uneven
ridiculously large;
he would have said
something about that.

His Rotary watch (a birthday present
from mum twenty years earlier)
was unfastened from his hand
and given to me,
congealed, on a worn leather strap,
still keeping the beat,
leaving a white patch on his wrist.

Moving Out After 100 Years

They pinned a white notice board
with long steel nails
into the flanks of the old house,
unaware of the screams only I could hear.
All these forty-five winters passed in a wink of an eye;
time taking all the people that loved it,
until left behind was only I.

Money can start a fire from ice,
or paint a fresco on sand ridden beaches,
fill deserts with crushed broken glass
kill and get away with it.

This family house, over 100 years,
will be disembowelled – all its entrails
deposited in a skip and recycled.
Mum will never make another fresh jasmine necklace
to hang round the statue of Our Lady.
Kids of my youth have been kidnapped by time.

All's silent as I carry garbage bags full of memories
to the transport lorry waiting outside.
I look back each time
I shut the door behind,
wishing it wasn't the last time,
the last summer I would hear
Cicadas rubbing their wings, into a mega buzz,
or watch colourful lizards like rainbows
rushing from shade into sun, into light.

My Great Aunt's House at Zejtun

My soul melted in the walls
and half of me had died,
like the well's gelid stones
in the courtyard when night falls.

Low arches touched my head,
each time I bowed, it seemed
in reverence to centuries
born on this four poster bed.

History spoke from picture frames,
when men wore bowler hats;
scowled deep through waxed moustache,
long gone in twenty decades.

Like film star macho men
with hats tilted on one side,
a cigarette between the fingers
as if the world belonged to them.

When the last key locked the door
memories screamed inside,
children's laughter died in silence,
ghostly footprints marked the floor.

Paul the Meticulous Fisherman

"Pawlu s-sajjied"[1], as he was nicknamed was a quiet lad.
Every Sunday morning he would clad in a beige suit and tie,
shine his shoes with spit, like soldiers in the army.
He was neat, in fact his other nickname, *"Pawlu l-fitt"*[2].
So meticulous in his work, preached to all how life was so ridiculous.
His walk was a rhythmic sway, of self confidence
stopping to observe the sea and the weather like all good fishermen.
It only seems like yesterday,
Pawlu was shouting himself hoarse: *"Lampuki friski, hajjin hajjin".*[3]
I often wonder how on earth no one realised he was in deep crisis,
deeper than the sea from where he caught us fresh fish every day.
His *luzzu*, *Santa Maria* was berthed at Spinola Bay.
Now it's gone, like him leaving an empty space,
only a buoy to mark its place.
Now he no longer shouts, "*Friski, hajjin hajjin* "
and the mornings are drear without his yellow smile.
When my dog ran out into the street last year
Pawlu gave chase and brought him back safe.
The *Santa Maria*[4] was red, black and yellow
painted in honour of St. Julian the village patron saint.
It would chug out happily from the bay, sometimes moon rising
every evening for many summery decades, as many as I can recollect,
rippling through the reflected white light of a dimming sunset.
Then he would whistle an unknown tune,
until his silhouette became one with dusk.
He lived with his old widowed mother, *Giuseppa*;
everyone knew she dotted on him, her only son.

She came back from early morning mass
one day and found him hanging from the neck.
The rope was tied by a fisherman's knot from the stairs' railings.
The doctor came first, then *Dun Karm*[5], the Parish priest.
Pawlu left us without a single word, his *luzzu* only a ghostly memory.
Now the moon rises on an empty quiet bay.

---

[1] Paul the meticulous fisherman.
[2] Paul the meticulous man.
[3] Dolphin fish, fresh, alive, alive.
[4] The boat is named St. Mary.
[5] Fr. Charles.

Rocky Vale

I was here as a child dreaming about adulthood:
"If only I was a grown-up, I would be free to steal
all happiness from the cauldron of life,
forget about having to eat boiled eggs,
or having cod liver oil forced down my throat".
Life then was played forward and backwards
on chalk-drawn boxes on a pavement,
where we seemed to balance our fortunes.
The rocks of the valley have been hewn away
by caterpillars that do not turn into butterflies.
Karmena[1], the farmer's wife, now breathes asthmatically up tarmac hills
into mists of fumes that corrupt the whiteness of her fresh eggs.
In the old days, I used to wait like a black panther
ready for attack as she approached within shooting range
of the balloon missile filled with water
that made her shriek and drop the wicker basket.
It was like the whole galaxy had rolled downhill
onto plush green turf still wet from night's dew.
Since then, birds have lost their nests in the trees
and people live in concrete-like prisons.
Keys are no longer left in the locks,
hearts have hardened, so Valentine comes only on the 14th,
and material things are all that's significant.
Time ebbs furtively away as if it doesn't want to hurt us,
leaving memories hanging like portraits.

---

[1] *Karmena* (Josephine)

Poppies

Multitudes of red lips
gasping at the wind;
like hungry mouths
wanting to be kissed.

Sunset steals the breeze
mobilising night's shadows,
over a Seven-Up float,
white cream on chocolate satin.

The red across the field
flows simultaneously,
like a blooded wave in a stadium
splashing from a giant wound -
against concrete apartments.

Sunset is colourless.
The night cannot be trusted.
Children are awake after 8 p.m.
in their lifeless cages.
Soon these poppies
will only be in their dreams.

Remnants of a Village

The old village used to smell
of fresh fish and sea lettuce,
of seawater stored in barrels
where fish were cleaned and washed.

The *luzzi*[1] are all departing
but not on fishing trips
to catch *lampuki*[2],
but on harbour cruises for tourists.

Ports are no longer made
from aging pebbles where crabs
used to build their den,
and little prawns tickled
children's toes as they cooled
their feet in the warm summer sea.
It's all luxurious yachts,
reserved for only those who could afford
flooded by artificial lights.

When the wind angers
the rest of the elements,
it's no longer like it's blowing kisses,
rather it's like it hisses:
"The past has passed,
no place for the past ..."

When the first rain falls,
the poppies and clover
will be gone from the fields,
where new concrete cages stand.
More trophies for the millionaires:
the red and green is only in artificial lights.

---

[1] *Luzzi* are traditional and colourful Maltese fishing boats

[2] *Lampuki* (Dolphin Fish), a traditional Maltese dish, which is very much sought after by tourists during the months of September, October and November, perhaps even later weather permitting.

The Straw Hat

Decades seemed to burst
from each crevice in the attic,
where the straw hat lay
on a dusty rocking chair.

Steel cobwebs chained
to breezes swayed,
like mama's hair
threads of shiny silver grey.

I remember her wearing it,
to hide from the sun;
now in permanent shade,
never to be worn again.

It's of sentimental value,
but who will care?
When I'm gone someone
will stuff it in a garbage bag.

And winds will howl
through fissured walls
like lone wolves,
that vanish in cotton mists.

The Green Boat

Inside it my youth juggles with the ghosts
frozen in the scent of weather-beaten wood.
Through its gaping crevices
I see the rust of the anchor
bleeding around a fossilized starfish.
Seagulls make a cacophonic melody
as if teasing humans for their limitations;
proud of their natural potential
to fly, float and walk on land.
This time capsule of youth is shattered
by the gasman, *Spiru*[1] hooting his horn,
a weekly wakeup call for his customers.
Those summers are now like some forgotten tale
when fresh fish glittered in their armoured scales
and time hung on the fishing line,
sinking into an abyss of green before it could age.
Wet fingers were cut easily by nylon thread,
but no blood was ever drawn.
Youth was invincible, I couldn't be hurt.
Now, I am mortal again,
the pain excruciating from just being human.

---

[1] *Spiru* is short for *Spiridione.*

The Waiting Room

In the waiting room made of lime stone
the lawyers are blank faces.
With black, chequered suits, white ties;
pale, like the ghosts haunting this house.

Time waves away the centuries;
centuries fall away to the clock's tick tock, tick tock,
the wind screeches through fissured walls.
Icy draughts seep through rock hard chairs.

The cold justice meted out
snaps sharply from a photocopier,
letter after letter, after letter after letter
to match the boring skies polluted with diesel.

The secretary's pink tight blouse
matches the slacks hugging her curves,
as she moves to a Brazilian rhythm,
glancing to see if she is being admired.

Then sits crossing her legs her ample flanks
filling the chair, her jellified assets
spilling over her computer, knowledge undisputed,
whilst conducting her boss's warfare.

Silence is only broken by the occasional
electric doors swishing open or shut,
like the curtains on a stage
of so many incredible life sagas.

People sleep their chins slammed into their chests,
like they're already dead, behind them
endless files stand like tomb stones,
commemorating nothing but useless strife.

Dreaming About My Home Village

Every time I dream,
my dream drifts to my home village,
where I grew,
when in those quiet days
the church bells only chimed
the waking of a new day.
When the streets were a holy place
and children could play safe
and only the boogey man was a danger.
The quaint houses were coloured gray,
yellow, green or fuchsia pink,
and little wooden windows
every evening lit like beaming eyes.

Every time I dream,
there's my little house, its shutters green
overlooking my Spinola Bay[1],
where the sea teased its pebbly shores
with sing song gentleness
that shushed silence into more.
When every early risen dawn
fishermen made their door to door calls,
with their glittering catch,
hollering proudly: "*hajjin, hajjin, friski hajjin*",[2]
that soon became our wake-up call;
instead of a battery operated alarm clock
that set one in a robotic mood.
When at the end of each day
as the sun plunged its red hot head into the deep,
their multi-coloured *luzzi*[3] chugged rhythmically away,

out of the picturesque bay,
when even darkness was still safe
and it was customary for people
to leave door keys in the locks.

Every time I dream
of winter as it used to be;
when the wind composed love songs
to our virgin trees
were children in the streets ran playfully;
their pink flushed faces smeared
with muddy soil from freshly fallen rains
that leaked from farmers' fields;
where potatoes and fresh broad beans
grew in multitudes awaiting harvesting.
When Christmas came,
it came with Christ a new born child,
when in those days the soul came first
and all seemed bathed in haloed light.
There was no revelling,
the joy we knew was at midnight Mass
in the traditional alter boy's sermon.
Then, all house decorations had cribs
and soft lights on freshly cut pine
that made Christmas an aromatic affair.
In spring, when winter slipped
into the warming air,
it was visible in the wayside
where waving poppies bled red
like a glowing face of healthy joy.

Every time I dream,
of my little village
there are no gray concrete-like prisons
of endless rows of new apartments,
soulless eye-sores and tasteless buildings
polluting my quaint little fishing village.
There are no fumes from belching buses,
or noise pollution besieging our quiet,
or the frantic pace of life
which has stolen all blissful moments
of quiet harmony;
when we could still hear and see our thoughts
and children lived in a safe environment.
When I dream now,
It's all a nightmare about an unrecognizable town
with traffic signs flashing the warning:
"PLEASE TURN BACK
YOU ARE NOW ENTERING
WHAT'S NO LONGER HEAVEN
BUT HELL INSTEAD!"

---

[1] *Spinola* is the name of one of the Grandmasters of the Knights of the Order of St. John's who governed the Maltese islands. The only existing palace, Spinola Palace in St. Julian's was named after him.

[2] *Hajjin* (alive); *friski* (fresh).

[3] *Luzzi*: Very colourful Maltese traditional fishing boats.

To My Fishing Village

No longer does the hoarse fishmonger
shout at the crack of dawn – *Lampuki hajjin, hajjin*![1]
The voice has been drowned by pneumatic hammers
to make way for a new hotel that must kill competitors.
Fresh fish is only available in restaurant freezers.

I can still see myself catching caterpillars,
climbing almond trees at Spinola Palace gardens,
now raped by the erection of Portomaso apartments.
I watched them turn from cocoons into Cabbage White,
blew softly on their unfolding wings to dry.

Attired in fancy running lights
the village is fossilised beneath concrete cages.
Kids are now men and men have turned to compost.
We are shadows of moving clouds,
vanishing with gusts of wind;
like the old tramp with the lame dog,
Spiru,[2] the paraffin man who died of cancer,
and the young fisherman's son,
who hanged himself from the stairs' railings.

The night sky is clear from dust –
the hurricanes of falling debris subside
into a silence that is solely inside the heart;
the orange light is only in dreams.

---

[1] Dolphin fish, alive, alive!
[2] *Spiru* is short for Spiridione.

Down Memory Lane

Sunset bent over the sea
of the poppy-filled field
arms unfolding orange rays.
I was nine or ten
walking into the faded dream
with my late aunt, Mary
through *Swieqi* Valley,
now buried beneath urban concrete.
Houses made of dry stone or cement
a cluster of white mixed with black,
tarmac ridden roads bleed black pollution,
many a sojourn for broken families
and distressed hearts.

Those were the bygone days
that now seem to have only been written in fairy tales.
I can no longer see blood-red soil
wet from first Autumn rains,
neither the chameleons
which used to cross my path in slow motion,
unafraid, unaware of men's greed;
the green yellow striped caterpillars
which magically wove themselves into cocoons;
farmhouses revelling with their barking dogs
the cocks' early morning wake up calls,
fresh eggs sold from wicker baskets
of a dozen each – some white some tan;
those evening tinkling bells beckoning the faithful
to the little chapel of Our Lady of the Immaculate Conception,
where I spent many a day as an altar boy.
Father Eugenio's gentle smile seems only like yesterday
as I poured rose wine into his silver chalice.
At home to a nightly quiet I would fall asleep
to the whispering murmur,
my parents reciting the rosary.

Everything then was like magic,
and children were taught
they were brought into this world by boat,
from far away unknown lands.
I was told by mother I came one stormy night,
travelling in a powerful sailing ship
steered by the great Columbus himself.
It was a miracle we made it to harbour
and I often wondered how I had survived?
When someone died, we were told he went to heaven,
the boogey man would carry away naughty children;
ladybirds were a sign of good luck,
so I picked the spotted creatures
that speckled with their red and black
white clothes hanging on our roof
to free them in the fields,
so my good luck would be twice fold.

We were happier with fewer and little things,
played with carton boxes converting them
into make-belief house or castle,
where we stored our dreams and aspirations.
Time did not run away from us then,
but stood still giving us more time to play,
allowing us to indulge in our innocence
our carefree life full of health and youth.
Summer holidays seemed forever then
until the new generation of evil,
greedy for money and political corruption
came like a wave of destruction
obliterating all in its path.
That's when time ran away
turning fabled dreams to nightmares.

Mama's Last Appassionata

Beethoven's *Appassionata* reverberated
sweeping from wall to wall,
as I stood silent in the hall,
thinking she'll never play this tune any more.

Music scores lay open where she'd last played
with gusto, love and pain
when her arthritic fingers
touched down heavily on every note,
like an uncontrollable weight.

Recalled how her frail figure would emerge
smiling into the sun filled hall,
as I knocked gently on the glass door,
almost afraid of smoldering the tune,
now realizing this scene was a *déjà vu*.

Outside, now a cacophony of sounds
far from Beethoven, Mozart or Bach,
a pollution of noise drowned the past,
all that was noble of value that lasts.

Those early summer mornings
when *Ix-Xejka*[1] limped up the porch
fresh *sargu*[2] in hand; his dog waited on the stairs,
as he wrapped the fish in newspaper,
then hobbled away to our next door neighbour.

The house had stood strong through decades and more
its walls like a fortress now thick with moss;
crevices now empty of crickets that chirped,
each time the summer night crept gently from light
while mama's fingers played us a lullaby.

Beethoven's *Appassionata* reverberated
through these double built walls,
my refuge for decades from spring to the fall;
now this last melody as the curtains are drawn.

---

[1] *Ix-Xejka* was a nickname of an old fisherman, *Karmnu* (Charles) who lived in a very small room with his small black dog close to the author's house.

[2] *Sargu* (White Seabream).

Il-Kuncizzjoni
(Our Lady of the Immaculate Conception Chapel)

Epilogue

Pooch
October 1999 – February 2011

Of My Life

My life started in October 1999. I was adopted by a family with children. All was well while I was a pup, but as soon as I grew in size, the children turned nasty and played awful tricks on me. I had to find somewhere to hide to avoid being tortured. One day, one of the kids became extremely nasty, pulling my tail and my ears very savagely. I only growled at him and barked but he went and lied to my master telling him that I had almost bitten him. That was the end of that – before I knew it, I was packed in the luggage booth of their car and abandoned on the road, far away from home.

I trudged the streets endlessly in search of food and water. Many times, I had to fight other dogs in order to survive. Sometimes I was beaten and kicked. People shooed me away because of my shabby appearance. My coat was light beige and therefore dirt was conspicuous. I spent nights out in the cold and rain, trying to find shelter under parked vehicles. Then I became very ill. I noticed a huge lump growing on my left flank. My ears were itching and hurting and my eyes were always watery. My strength was fading fast. I knew that the end was near. I had contracted Sand fly, a disease that comes after being bitten by a Sand fly, which lives in hot climates like that of Malta.

That night I set out for the last journey, hoping that some kind soul would take pity and at least give me a place where I could die in peace. That night was when I had a good turn of fortune. I was walking along the road at the most busy traffic arteries in the city centre, outskirts of St. Julian's. It was a hot summer night in July 2000. My eyes were watering; I could hardly see where I was going. I was following my instinct, using my nose and ears and keeping to the side of the road as hundreds of cars sped past me. I was seriously considering crossing the road to put an end to my miserable life.

Suddenly, a car stopped. A man and a woman got out of the vehicle. By now, I had lost all faith in humans because I had experienced so much cruelty, but my instinct told me that these young couple meant well. I crossed over to their car. They actually let me in on the back seat. I was taken to their home and given food and water and the next day, I was taken to the dog's sanctuary. At first, I thought that I had gone from the frying pan into the fire but the man, whose name now I knew to be Raymond promised me he would not allow anyone to harm me and swore he would take care of me.

An advert was put in the newspaper in an attempt to find my owners, but of course, I knew this was a waste of time. My owners weren't looking for me. They probably hoped I was dead. After a week at the dog's sanctuary, Raymond kept his promise and came back for me. I could hardly contain my joy and emotions and knew that finally I had found someone who really cared.

I guess Ray thought I'd be happier with other dogs. He took me to his friend's house where there were three dogs. He could see pretty quickly that I was a good dog as I got along well with Pippa, a boxer, Rex an Alsatian and Little, a miniature Schnauzer. I was quite happy there and relaxed. No more perking up my ears every time I heard a sound that might be a child with sticky fingers tugging my tail as if it were the lever of an old well. Ray came every day and took me out for walks. He took me to a kind vet who gave me injections to cure me from the Sand fly. I started regaining my strength and the lump on my left flank was soon gone. Even my ears did not itch and my eyes felt better. My new master could not take me to his home because he lived in an apartment where dogs and cats were not allowed.

The happiest period came about after almost a year when Ray came for me and took me to his mother's home, a very kind old woman in her late seventies. I lived there for three years. I used to help her climb up and down the stairs as she had terrible mobility problems. What a difference it made to feel like I was helping someone. Life had a purpose. In the meantime, my master bought a house and he took me there to live with him.

However, our happiness in the new house was short-lived. In 2004, I noticed that something was wrong. Raymond's appearance was changing. He was losing weight and was ill most of the time. Then he started losing his strength. I had to be careful that he didn't fall over when he tried to walk me. That year, until the end of 2005 was the most painful period of my life. My master had been diagnosed with a terrible disease called Hodgkin's Disease. I noticed that my mistress was often crying desperately while my master spent long periods in hospital undergoing various tests.

One particular night, my instinct was alerted by danger. It was not the danger I had faced so often time from other dogs or humans – it was something much worse. The house became extremely cold and I knew that what I was facing was neither human nor animal. It was a shadow, black with empty sockets in the place of the eyes – it was Death in person come to fetch my master. I could smell it and even though I had never encountered it, I knew it was there. I felt helpless and would have rather faced a savage wolf than this entity. However, I felt I owed it to my master, at least to give this entity a good fight. I came out of my basket and using my deepest and most fearsome growl, I stood there face to face with it. I paced and barked and howled all night until I had no more strength in my voice. Then all was quiet. The coldness had disappeared almost as if a gust of wind had carried it away. I had won this battle and knew the danger was gone.

Only minutes later, my mistress, Angela, got a telephone call from the hospital asking her to go to my master's side, as he was not well. But by then, I already knew that the danger was gone and that he would survive. Pity I could not communicate in human language otherwise I would have told dear Angela that she needn't fear, for I had scared Death away from the house.

Consequently my master was advised by his doctors that his only chance to beat cancer was to undergo chemotherapy. I would have loved to be close by his bedside, but I was not allowed into the hospital. When he came home, I spent long nights watching him closely and noticed his otherwise pleasant face turn into contortions of pain. But even then, his hand would often gently reach out to fondle my head. "Don't worry, Pooch. I'm going to beat this. No disease is going to take me down," Raymond said. Just hearing his usual strong, voice reassured me that he was going to be all right.

Now I am proud to be part of his foundation, Paranormal Investigations & Research Foundation (Malta G. C.) I always accompany him on his onsite investigations. I can sense danger before humans as my sense of smell and hearing is even better than that of other dogs because I am partially blind.

Unfortunately, my health hasn't been too good lately. It doesn't help that I'm almost totally blind. Last year I fell down the stairs. I was following my master as we came down from the roof. It was time for my supper. Without my sight, I miscalculated the last three or four steps and went through the staircase railing. I fell on my hind legs and being 35 kilos, and having arthritis, the fall caused me great pain. I was walking funny and unable to go for long walks for about two weeks, but my master used to massage my legs with some special ointment and gave me special pills for the pain until I became well again. A physiotherapist used to come every week to give me special treatments and exercise.

The walks however had to be shortened. As we headed for the car, I'd stop and pull on the leash, turning to let Raymond know that I couldn't go on. He never argued with me. "That's okay," he'd say. "You've done well to get out this far." I knew he was trying to make me feel better, as if nothing had changed from the endless walks we used to have.

However, that was not the end of my troubles. Soon in November 2011, I developed an inflammation in my eyes. Again, I was miserable and disorientated for quite a few weeks. But my master's perseverance and the eye drop medicines prescribed by Dr. Trevor Zammit made me well again.

However, deep down I sensed that I was nearing the end of the road. I was worried because I knew how dearly my master loved me and kept thinking of all the emptiness and void I would leave behind me in the house. One Sunday morning after breakfast, my master noticed a drop of blood on the kitchen floor. That same morning, after my favourite walk at Pembroke, he took me to the St. Francis Animal Welfare Centre. I had been there before. This time was different. Raymond spoke to the vet with a slight tremble in his voice. "Is he going to be okay?" Trevor tried to console Raymond, "Let's take a look before you get too worked up about things, shall we?"

The vet put me on a table and started to roll a strange-wheeled thing on my tummy, which was wired to a computer screen. There were three vets and I could see from their faces and that of my master that things were not looking too good.

That was the worst Sunday I can recall. I noticed that at times Ray kept wiping tears from his eyes. The next day we went for our usual walk at Pembroke. As we returned to the car, Raymond sat behind the wheel staring at the wonderful view of which we had enjoyed together for so many years. His hand was fondling my head more strongly than usual and suddenly he turned, gave me a huge hug and muttered something about the possibility it would be the last time we would visit Pembroke again. I noticed he was crying. Something was definitely terribly wrong with me.

Pembroke was special because my master's childhood was very much tied to this place, which lies on the outskirts of the fishing village of St. Julian, where he was born and lived for 30 years. It used to belong to the British Services and consists of a huge span of countryside lying next to a rocky seaside. In Spring, I recall Ray taking pictures of the hundreds of different types of colourful wild flowers growing there. It was peaceful and I recall my very first walk there I got so carried away with the wide expanse that Ray lost sight of me and got very worried. However, I wasn't going to let him go away without me so I took a short cut and waited for him next to the car. Ray was very angry with me, which is very rare. If we were not to come here anymore, I would miss my walks and my best friends, Spotty, Patches and Lara.

From our walk, we went straight to the vet again. My master took off my collar and I was lifted onto a stretcher. The area of my tummy was shaved and so were my wrists. All this time, my master fondled my head and pressed me to his chest, at times so close I could hear his beating heart. Then it was time for some sort of injection, and after that, I don't remember anything.

When I came to, my master was waiting for me. I was in great pain, but put on a courageous front and walked out of the vet's clinic. My master was very pleased. I recall my favourite vet, Dr. Delphine saying to him "Pooch is a tough old cookie."

When I arrived home I was grateful, but the pain in my tummy was excruciating and despite my attempts to hide the discomfort, I could not lie down to rest. My master stayed up with me every night after that day. He was there all the time, 24 hours a day. I was fed fresh meat, salmon, liver, chicken and so many other delicious meals. But I also noticed that my appetite was fading – pity to let all that good food go to waste! I tried hard to eat. "Good boy," was a constant refrain from Ray when I managed to get a mouthful down. Our walks had to stop completely and even simply going around the corner from my home was becoming harder and harder, as my strength was fading fast and the bones on my haunches were protruding due to the great amount of weight I had lost in the three weeks after the operation.

I knew, the time had come for us to part. I made various signals to my master that the time was ripe, and knew that he was aware of this too. My appetite was practically gone. I had always been a big eater, so I, more than anyone else knew I was dying slowly. My hind legs had little or no strength and in fact, Ray slept next to me on a very uncomfortable sofa and would wake up constantly at night to help me change positions. He even brought me fresh milk to drink and water. The vet had already warned him that the biopsy on the tumour found on my spleen had turned out to be malignant. "It's a matter of time," he said and explained that usually a dog in my condition lived between three to six months.

My master seemed inconsolable but he is the type of person that never gives up. Perhaps his own personal fight against cancer made him a tougher nut to crack. He found a special dog treat supplement on the internet and bought some packets for me. Apparently, this phenomenal dog food boosted the immune system and by taking regular dosages, it helped dogs like myself to fight cancer and in some cases lengthened their life span.

My master didn't waste any time ordering the product, which was called K9 Plus. It was manufactured and available only in the USA. When the couriers went to pick up the package, the customs officer refused to allow it into the country. It was then that Raymond started making a series of phone calls. The first people he spoke to were the customs. "You must be joking or you must have never had a pet in your life. Do you realize that by withholding this package, you are killing my dog?" It was when I heard those words that I realized what was happening. My master was very livid with anger. But that wasn't the end of the sad saga. The next hurdle was getting the green light from the Port Health. Ray wrote to the director and Government vet including all the specifications of the K9. Days passed before the approval was granted, but then the Trade Department wanted Ray to apply for an import licence for a 200-gram packet of dog treats. Raymond was being pushed to the limits of his temper and I was afraid of that because I had heard quite a few stories about how he got himself into trouble in his younger days because of this. He used every contact and influence he had to combat the bureaucratic system. Soon the leading English newspaper he used to work for came to his assistance and sent a photographer and reporter to our house to take pictures of my master with Angela and myself. I am ever so grateful for all he did in an attempt to save my life and render the last moments more pleasant. But cancer does not wait for bureaucracy.

The 16th February 2011 was my last day at my home with my beloved family. Ray's eyes were constantly filled with tears as he leaned down to give me a bowl of food. Angela tried to comfort him. "You've given Pooch a good life. Just think of how mangy he looked when we first found him at the side of the road." Angela kept hugging me and kissing me. Then she, too, began to cry. Ray gained his composure, but as humans like to say, "It was the calm before the storm." At mid-day a nurse from my St. Francis Animal Welfare Centre came with a van and I was lifted carefully in. The journey took about 10 minutes. My master followed with Michael, a friend in another car. When we got to the clinic, I was once again lifted gently onto a waiting stretcher and taken inside. Dr. Delphine was waiting for me. She probably had seen many dogs go through what I was about to endure. She was not the usual jolly person I was used to. Instead, her pretty face was contorted with sadness. That is when Ray began to cry uncontrollably.. I had never seen my master so distraught not even when he suffered excruciating pain from his cancer and the side effects of the chemotherapy.

I was not worried about myself really, because I knew that my journey crossing over Rainbow Bridge would be brief and painless.

At this point, I looked forward to my ill health and my blindness fading away. My question was: what was to become of my beloved master after I was gone – would he recover? We had spent so many years together. We had become family.

He took me with him everywhere, even when he visited his clients. At times, I used to wait for him in the car. I sat in front on the passenger seat, and guarded the vehicle till he returned. I remember when we used to be late for an appointment, Raymond used to put his foot down on the accelerator. My head used to be in his lap, so to make sure, he wouldn't speed too much I used to dig my chin deeper into his lap and make funny groaning noises to attract his attention. I remember he used to pat my head, smile and tell me, "all right Buddy, I know you don't like me speeding, I'll slow down".

I used to lie down by his side when he was terribly ill and in great pain. And when he became well again, I used to lie happily by his side while he was studying or writing, even when he was giving creative writing classes. I remember, the special Barbecue evenings in summer when I used to go up on the roof with him while he prepared the barbecue and all the good food and delicious sausages. They were all special times I will never forget. One thing for sure, Raymond made me immortal when my story and photos were published on the newspaper. And from what I have overheard, Ray isn't through with the authorities yet and will be making several appearances on National television as well. Last but not least, I also remember he promised to dedicate his book of poems to me and publish my autobiography in it as well. All these wonderful memories rushed through my mind like a fast-forwarded video, but as they say, all good things must come to an end sometime.

Dr. Delphine spoke to me gently as she injected something inside me. "This is only going to hurt for a second." It made me feel very sleepy. My master kept repeating softly "I love you," over and over again - as if I didn't know! I was already fading, when the vet gave me another injection, this time in my chest … and all was quiet and calm … there was no more storm.

An Apology to Pooch

Your 19-inch collar weighed in my hands
like it had never weighed before,
still warm with your name inscribed on the medallion.
I placed it in a box and hid it in the attic.
Perhaps I put you through unnecessary pain,
should never have allowed the operation,
the seven inch cut in your belly
that caused you excruciating pain,
contorting your brown blind eyes
that never lost their loving gaze,
not even for a moment.
I want to apologise my friend
for the pain I caused you towards the end,
when you were in agony and I was angry;
when the K9 immune treats were withheld by customs,
the only hope for your salvation.
I want to apologise for my inability to put up a fight,
not using enough force to give you your last chance.
When your cancer took away your huge appetite
and you kept turning your head away, even from fried liver
my anger increased – I was losing the battle.
I want to apologise for being weak
when I should have been strong
for having put you to sleep, you of all friends,
my very best, who was crucial in my coming back from cancer.
I repaid you by allowing the vet
to pierce your heart with poison.
Yet you placed your head in my hand,
your last gesture, as if I was your saviour;
your unconditional love, your faith in me to the very end
relentless.

It was as if you were telling me:
"Please let me go – it's time – don't worry".
And you crossed Rainbow Bridge without me.
When I look back, I cannot come to terms with your departure,
wish my breathing was controlled by a switch
so I could turn it off to take away the pain.
I apologise my friend for being such a coward.

Raymond Fenech
February 2011

All funds raised by the book will be in aid of the Association for Abandoned Animals

Raymond Fenech

Raymond Fenech embarked on his writing career as a freelance journalist for three leading political newspapers, and later as a news reporter with The Times and Sunday Times of Malta. More recently, he set up an in house advertising agency for a major travel agency, which he managed and then helped launch The Globe Trotter, a travel magazine, which he also edited. Ray's poetry, essays, articles and short stories have been published in twelve countries and he has published research on Malta ghosts in the International Directory of the Most Haunted Places by Penguin Books, USA. The author is also a qualified paranormal investigator and the founder director of the Paranormal Investigations & Research Foundation (Malta). He has recently graduated with a bachelor's degree in creative writing and parapsychology and is pursuing a course in poetry therapy. The author is also a qualified copywriter listed with the Institute of Copywriters, UK. He conducts creative writing classes for both children and adults.

Lightning Source UK Ltd.
Milton Keynes UK
UKOW052309140112

185428UK00001B/3/P